Alpha

Published in North America by Alpha North America, 2275 Half Day Road Suite 185, Deerfield, IL 60015

Alpha Team Guide*

This edition first printed by Alpha North America in 2015

Printed in the United States of America

ISBN 978-1-938328-70-1

1 2 3 4 5 6 7 8 9 10 Printing/Year 18 `17 16 15

Contents

Section 1
Training

Training 1
How to Host
an Alpha
Small Group

The aim of this session is to give you all the tools you will need to host or help in the Alpha small group.

'You know, brothers and sisters, that our visit to you was not a failure. We had previously suffered and been insulted in Philippi, as you know, but **with the help of our God** we dared to **tell you his gospel** in the face of strong opposition. For **the appeal we make does not spring from error or impure motives, nor are we trying to trick you.** On the contrary, we speak as those approved by God to be **entrusted with the gospel.** We are **not trying to please people** but God, who tests our hearts. You know we never used flattery, **nor did we put on a mask** to cover up greed – God is our witness. We were not looking for human praise, not from you or anyone else.

As apostles of Christ we could have been a burden to you, but **we were gentle among you,** like a mother caring for her little children. **We loved you so much** that we were delighted to share with you **not only the gospel of God but our lives as well,** because you had become so dear to us. Surely you remember, brothers and sisters, our toil and hardship; **we worked night and day** in order not to be a burden to anyone while we preached the gospel of God to you.

You are witnesses, and so is God, of **how holy, righteous and blameless** we were among you who believed. For you know that we dealt with each of you as a father deals with his own children, **encouraging, comforting and urging you to live lives worthy of God**, who calls you into his kingdom and glory'

(1 Thessalonians 2:1–12)

The overall purpose of the small group, along with Alpha as a whole, is to bring people into a relationship with Jesus Christ by sharing the good news of 'the gospel' (1 Thessalonians 2:2, 4, 8).

- Jesus chose a group of twelve (Matthew 4:18–22)
- A group of about twelve is the ideal size: small enough that everyone can participate, big enough that there is no pressure to speak
- Each small group is made up of two hosts, two or three helpers and approximately eight guests

The three primary aims of the Alpha small group are to **love, learn** and **live.**

LOVE

Alpha is about sharing God's love through friendship

The gospel is ultimately about love.

- God's love for us (Romans 5:5)
- Our love for God (Luke 10:27)
- Our love for others (Mark 12:31)

'We loved you so much that we were delighted to share with you not only the gospel of God but *our lives as well'* (1 Thessalonians 2:8).

The greatest thing you can do as a host or helper is to share your life with your guests.

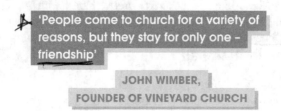

'People come to church for a variety of reasons, but they stay for only one – friendship'

JOHN WIMBER,
FOUNDER OF VINEYARD CHURCH

Hosting a small group is similar to hosting a small party:

- Arrange the room beforehand: with a circle of chairs for each group and perhaps a small coffee table in the middle with easy access in and out

- Create a welcoming atmosphere: put on some background music and think about the lighting

- Welcome the guests as they arrive: find out their name (give them a name badge) and introduce them to one another

- Cater for the needs of each guest: make sure they have food, drink and are aware of the facilities on-site

- Put your guests at ease: avoid heavy or religious topics and facilitate conversation

- Finish on time: have a finish time so guests know when they can leave and stick to it

- Remember: no pressure, no follow up, no charge

Role of the host:
- To greet newcomers to the group
- To introduce guests to one another
- To facilitate the discussion

Role of the helper:
- To look after the needs of guests
- To handle administration for the group
- Don't say too much in the discussion

Making guests feel at home and relaxed is important throughout Alpha, but particularly for the first session.

LEARN

Alpha is a chance to ask anything

> '(People) are never so likely to settle a
> question rightly as when they discuss it
> freely'
>
> **THOMAS MACAULAY**

- No question is too simple
- No question is too hostile

The model for the Alpha small group is not teacher-pupil, but host-guest. It is vital to give guests the opportunity to respond to what they have heard and to ask questions in a safe, non-threatening environment.

Groups can be ruined by one of two things:

- Weak leadership – not being properly prepared and allowing one person to do all the talking

- Dominant leadership – doing all the talking, instead of giving guests the freedom to speak and to say what is on their mind

Use all the Tools to prep
- *Questions of Life*
- *This Team Guide*
- *Searching Issues*

FOUR TIPS FOR HOSTING A GREAT DISCUSSION:

1. BE ENCOURAGING

'For you know that we dealt with each of you as a father deals with his own children, encouraging [and] comforting' (1 Thessalonians 2:11–12).

- Every point of view is a view with a point   *affirming*
  answers
  - most people worry about looking stupid   *and questions*
  - encourage everyone who speaks that their point of view is valid and important: 'how interesting!'

- Enable everyone to participate
  - avoid giving your opinion but throw the question to the group
  - if someone states their opinion, encourage others to participate: 'What does anyone else think?'

- Use open questions: *Closed*
  - not 'do you think Jesus is God?', but 'who do you think Jesus is?'
  Open-ended.

- Set the bar low:
  - not 'how often do you pray?', but 'has anyone here ever prayed?'

- Remember that people process information in different ways:
  - what do you think … about Jesus?   *Two primary*
  - what do you feel … about Jesus?   *questions*

- Don't be afraid of silence: the guests are exploring deep questions

- However, if the silence becomes awkward:
  - rephrase the question
  - go in a different direction
  - put forward a controversial viewpoint

2. BE YOURSELF

'... the appeal we make does not spring from error or impure motives, nor are we trying to trick you ... you know we never used flattery, nor did we put on a mask' (1 Thessalonians 2:3, 5).

- Explain clearly what your roles are in the group
- If you don't know the answer, don't pretend you do!

3. BE PREPARED

'Always be prepared to give an answer to everyone who asks you to give the reason for the hope that you have' (1 Peter 3:15).

Exceptions to asking 'What does anyone else think?'

A. Questions of fact
- Eg, how many gospels are there?
- Eg, where are the toilets?

B. Direct questions
- Eg, why are you a Christian?
- Eg, when did it first make sense for you?

C. Difficult questions
- In the first session, make a note of everyone's questions
- If you don't know the answer, tell guests that you'll find out and get back to them next week

- Recommended reading: the *Searching Issues* book by Nicky Gumbel. Chapters include 'Why Does God Allow Suffering?', 'What About Other Religions?', 'Is There a Conflict Between Science and Christianity?', 'Is the Trinity Unbiblical, Unbelievable and Irrelevant?', 'What About the New Spirituality?', 'Does Religion Do More Harm Than Good?' and 'Is Faith Irrational?'

4. BE RESPECTFUL

'... But do this with gentleness and respect' (1 Peter 3:15).

- Avoid being patronising
  - guests may be new to Christianity, but they are not new to life
  - never underestimate guests' intelligence
  - never overestimate guests' knowledge
- The group is more important than the individual
- If someone is too talkative and dominates the group:
  - direct questions elsewhere in the group
  - if necessary talk to them outside the group and encourage them to hold back in order to allow others to contribute
  - if they are already a strong Christian, ask them to be a helper
  - if necessary, ask for help from your Head of Alpha or church pastor/priest/minister

LIVE

Alpha is an opportunity for guests to experience what it's like to live the Christian life, in the Christian community.

'For you know that we dealt with each of you as a father deals with his own children, encouraging, comforting and urging you to live lives worthy of God, who calls you into his kingdom and glory' (1 Thessalonians 2:11–12).

1. WORSHIP

Worship is a key part of Alpha – there are usually one or two songs led from the front before each talk

- Guests often find the singing the hardest part to engage with at the beginning, but it is often their favourite part by the end
- Emphasise that guests are welcome to participate if they would like to, but no one should feel any pressure to do so

2. PRAYER

Prayer undergirds everything we do on Alpha, from the beginning to the end.

- Before you begin
  - the weekly pre-session team prayer meeting is vital, a chance to pray for yourself, the team and the guests in your group
  - divide up the group between the hosts and helpers and commit to praying for each guest on a weekly basis

- From the front
  - the topic of prayer is introduced in Session 5 – 'How and Why Should I Pray?'
  - we avoid public prayer to avoid guests feeling uncomfortable
  - we don't say 'grace' or pray before the meal

- In your small group
  - you may want to offer to say a short closing prayer at the end of this discussion or in any of the subsequent sessions – 'Would anyone mind if I said a short prayer to finish?'
  - at some point you may feel it's appropriate to give your guests an opportunity to pray out loud
  - go around the group and ask each person if there's anything they'd like prayer for
  - a host should start with a very short prayer; long eloquent prayers may be impressive, but they discourage others from praying
  - give space for those who would like to pray, to do so
  - one of the helpers should not pray, to avoid putting pressure on any guests who may not want to pray
  - a host should finish with a short prayer

- It is important that the guests have experienced group prayer before the session 'Does God Heal Today?', where there will be an opportunity for the guests to pray for one another

....

....

....

....

3. THE BIBLE

Alpha seeks to introduce guests to reading the Bible for themselves.

- From the front
  - all of the Alpha talks are based on one or many passages from the Bible
  - reading the Bible is introduced in Session 6 – 'How and Why Should I Read the Bible?'

- In your small group
  - help guests in your group navigate around the Bible by finding references and page numbers for them
  - you may want to encourage guests to buy their own Bible and Bible reading guide, such as *30 Days*. You could also recommend the daily Bible in One Year commentary by Nicky Gumbel at alpha.org/bioy or listening to the Bible online
  - towards the end of the course guests may be interested in exploring the Bible further or joining a Bible study group

4. LIFESTYLE

'Surely you remember, brothers and sisters, our toil and hardship; we worked night and day in order not to be a burden to anyone while we preached the gospel of God to you' (1 Thessalonians 2:9).

- Hosting and helping is a commitment
- Commitment to attending training, attending each session and going on the weekend
- Commitment to the guests before, during and after Alpha: through friendship and in prayer
- Commitment despite disappointments

- Commitment to leadership: progression from guest to helper to host at the discretion of the Alpha head/church pastor

'You are witnesses, and so is God, of how holy, righteous and blameless we were among you' (v.10).

- Hosting and helping means trying to model the Christian life
- We're all on a journey and none of us is perfect
- But aim to be a model of Christian living
- Treatment of one another and behaviour in general
- Ultimately we want to point people to Christ, not ourselves

Remember that laughter is a key component of Alpha. Have fun and enjoy the journey.

Training 2
How to Pray on the Alpha Weekend

This is not the norm on the first few weeks...

The aim of this session is to give you all the tools you'll need to pray with and for the guests on the Alpha weekend.

> 'There are different kinds of gifts, but the same Spirit. There are different kinds of service, but the same Lord. There are different kinds of working, but the same God works all of them in everyone. Now to each one **the manifestation of the Spirit is given for the common good**. To one there is given through the Spirit the message of **wisdom**, to another the message of **knowledge** by means of the same Spirit, to another **faith** by the same Spirit, to another gifts of **healing** by that one Spirit, to another **miraculous powers**, to another **prophecy**, to another **distinguishing between spirits**, to another speaking in different kinds of **tongues**, and to still another the **interpretation of tongues**. All these are the work of one and the same Spirit, and **he gives them to each one**, just as he determines'
>
> **(1 CORINTHIANS 12:4-11)**

What is prayer ministry?
- The word 'ministry' is used in several different senses in the New Testament
- Ministry in the broadest sense means 'serving' others
- Prayer ministry means serving others through prayer, 'meeting the needs of others on the basis of God's

resources' (John Wimber)
- It is the activity of the Holy Spirit which transforms every aspect of Alpha
- 'Come Holy Spirit' ('Veni Sancte Spiritus') – the oldest prayer of the church
- We offer ourselves to God as his servants, and leave the rest to him

Small Group 1 (Saturday morning):
- This discussion is key to facilitating the rest of the weekend
- Read 1 Corinthians 12:4–11 verse by verse with the group; perhaps suggest that each person read one verse
- Ask guests what they think each of the spiritual gifts mentioned might mean
- Make sure you cover in particular the gift of prophecy and the gift of speaking in tongues as these come up in the talk 'How Can I Be Filled with the Holy Spirit?'
- Hosts and helpers should offer their opinions and experiences once the guests have shared theirs

How to pray:

1. RESPECT THE GUESTS

- Sit near your group so that you can easily pray for them
- Offer to pray for each member of your group in turn
  - men pray with men, women pray with women
- Ask if there is anything specific you can pray for
- They may want to pray a prayer of commitment to Jesus
  - you could use the prayer in the *Why Jesus?* booklet p.18
  - you could use your own prayer: sorry, thank you, please
- They may want to receive a gift of the Spirit

- Confidentiality is important
  - don't pray loudly, nor gossip with others
  - exceptions: if in doubt, seek the advice of your Head of Alpha or church pastor/priest/minister
- Explain what will happen

2. RELY ON THE SPIRIT

- Pray simple prayers: 'come Holy Spirit', 'thank you that you love [guest's name]'
- Trust in Jesus' promises: expect the Holy Spirit to come (Luke 11:13)
- Keep your eyes open: watch what is happening
- Avoid intensity: no special 'prayer voice', religious language, eccentricity
- Avoid laying unnecessary burdens on guests, eg lack of faith
- Avoid praying about sensitive subjects: relationships, children, jobs, money
- Avoid criticising other denominations or churches

'… the one who prophesies speaks to people for their strengthening, encouraging and comfort' (1 Corinthians 14:3).

3. ROOT YOURSELF IN THE BIBLE

- The Spirit of God and the Bible never conflict
- Build on the Bible's promises
  - freedom from guilt (Romans 8:1)
  - assurances of repentance (Psalm 51)
  - release from fear (Psalm 91)
  - God's guidance (Psalm 37:5)
  - power to overcome temptation (1 Corinthians 10:13)
  - peace in times of anxiety (Philippians 4:6–7)

4. RELAX AND TRUST GOD

- Ask: 'what do you sense is happening?' or 'do you sense God saying something?'
- Refuse to consider that 'nothing has happened'
- Hold on to God's promises
- Go on being filled with the Spirit (Ephesians 5:18)
- Warn against possible increased temptation
- Stay in touch

Section 2
Small
Group
Questions

HOSTS' AND HELPERS' PREPARATION

- Each job within the team is vitally important. If you are unable to do the job you've been given, please let the Alpha head know
- Please ensure that everyone goes to the hosts' meeting before the session – there are important notices and helpful reminders given each week

RUNNING ORDER SUGGESTIONS FOR A TYPICAL ALPHA SESSION

- **6.00 pm***
  Hosts' meeting for all hosts and helpers: everyone needs to be clear where their group is sitting for both the meal and discussion time

- **6.30 pm**
  When the hosts' meeting ends, hosts and helpers go to welcome their guests

- **6.30–7 pm**
  As guests arrive, the Alpha head should allocate them to a group, and introduce them to a runner who will show them to their group

  One host should stay with the group at all times and the other helpers and hosts can show guests where to pick up their meal. In practice, you may have friends who you want to chat to, but your group is your number one priority. You can catch up with your friends another time!

- **7 pm**
  Food should be served as quickly as possible to avoid long queues and allow small groups to talk during the mealtime. Money for the meal can be collected at the serving point (with a sign, 'Suggested Donation')

- **7.30 pm**
  Encourage guests to move their chairs if necessary in order to see the worship leader and speaker

- **8.30 pm**
  Talk ends. Swiftly get into your small group for the discussion time. Allocate the coffee serving to one of the helpers

- **9.20 pm**
  Make sure you finish on time after each session. As the discussion draws to a close, suggest going for a drink together and/or help guests who may be interested in buying books and resources

You may want to think about how people can purchase books from the recommended reading list, either by directing them online or selling books through your own bookshop. If you have a bookshop, we suggest opening during the meal and small group discussion.

*Running times have been given as a guide only

Is there
more to
life
than

this

1. Ensure that you have registered everyone in the group and that each person has a name badge

2. Serve drinks and snacks before beginning the discussion

3. Welcome everyone to the group

4. Introduce yourselves and explain your roles

5. Explain the format for each session and the number of sessions

6. Highlight: no pressure, no follow up, no charge

7. Explain the format and purpose of the small group discussion

8. Reassure the guests that you always finish on time

ICEBREAKERS

These games will enable the group to remember each other's names and get to know one another.

NAME GAME

- 'Everyone think of a positive adjective that starts with the same letter as your first name' eg 'Jovial John' or 'Happy Helen' OR 'Everyone think of a famous person with the same first name as you' eg 'Justin Bieber', 'Sandra Bullock'

- Start with the person on your left. They must say their name and positive adjective or celebrity name. The next person must say their name and adjective or celebrity name and that of the person before them

- Each person must try and repeat all the names of the guests preceding them from memory. The host is the last person to go and repeats the names of everyone in the group

- Be quick to help any guests who might find this more difficult

DESERT ISLAND GAME

- 'If you were stuck on a desert island and you could take one thing (not a person) with you and you already have the Bible and the complete works of Shakespeare, what would you take?'

- OR 'Which person from history would you like to be stuck in a lift with, and why?'

'HOW AND WHY DID YOU END UP COMING HERE TODAY?'

- This gives the rest of the group permission to say what they really think. Try to draw more out of guests if they are a bit hesitant. Start with the guest you think is most reluctant/hostile

'IF IT TURNED OUT THAT GOD EXISTED AND YOU COULD ASK ONE QUESTION, WHAT WOULD IT BE?'

- 'These are great questions'
- Write the questions down on a piece of paper with a view to coming back to them at the end of Alpha

Finish on time and carry on discussion elsewhere (café, kitchen) for those who want to.

Who is
Jesus

Welcome the group then go around and ask each person to introduce themselves briefly. Welcome any new guests, and ask them: 'How and why did you end up coming here today?' Pass around the registration list. Add any new names and contact details and correct any mistakes from the previous week.

QUESTIONS FOR DISCUSSION

1. Who do you think Jesus is?

2. When you think of Jesus what do you feel?

3. Before you heard the talk tonight, what was your concept of Jesus? Has it changed? If so, in what way?

4. What aspects of the evidence presented tonight did you find convincing/not convincing?

5. If you had a chance to meet Jesus, how would you feel and what would you say to him?

why did Jesus die

Introduce any new guests. Pass around the registration list. Add any new names and contact details and correct any mistakes from the previous session.

QUESTIONS FOR DISCUSSION

This is often the session when the subject of 'suffering' arises (see Searching Issues chapter 'Why Does God Allow Suffering?').

1. What do you think/how do you feel about the idea of forgiveness? What is it? Have you ever had to forgive anyone?

2. What do you think/how do you feel about the idea of guilt? Have you ever had to receive forgiveness? What does it take to receive God's forgiveness?

3. Do you think that sin is an out-dated subject?

4. What is your reaction to Jesus' death?

How can we have faith

Introduce any new guests. Pass around the registration list and amend if needed. This is a good session to mention the Alpha weekend for the first time. Give the dates to the guests.

QUESTIONS FOR DISCUSSION

You may find that guests have questions, for example, about other religions (see *Searching Issues* chapter 'What About Other Religions?').

1. How do you feel about the idea of a relationship with God?

2. Do you associate love or fear with God?

3. What do you think when you hear about people's lives being transformed as a result of coming to faith?

4. When it is said that Christianity will make a change in your character, how do you feel?

pray

**Why and
how do I**

This is a good session to encourage guests to attend the Alpha weekend. Mention the cost and the possibility of bursaries.

QUESTIONS FOR DISCUSSION

1. Have you ever tried praying? What happened?

2. What do you think about the idea of God answering prayer?

3. Can anyone describe a time when a 'coincidence' happened?

4. In the talk, various reasons for praying are given. Which of these do you relate to and why?

Why how I the and should read Bible

Remind the group about the Alpha weekend. Ask someone who has benefited from a previous one to describe their experience. Take further names and collect payment.

QUESTIONS FOR DISCUSSION

1. Has anyone here ever read the Bible? How did you get on?

2. Have you ever read a modern translation of the Bible?

3. Have you read anything in the Bible that has challenged an aspect of your beliefs or behaviour?

4. What do you feel about the suggestion that the Bible is a 'manual for life'?

How does God guide us

Arrange transport for the Alpha weekend if necessary.

QUESTIONS FOR DISCUSSION

1. In the last few weeks, has anyone had any experience that they think might be God guiding them?

2. How do you feel about the idea of God having a plan for you?

3. What are the ways that God speaks to people today? Have you experienced this?

4. What should we do if we believe we have made a mess of our lives?

Who
is the **Holy Spirit**

There is no small group discussion following this session.

What
does the
Holy Spirit do

QUESTIONS FOR DISCUSSION

Read 1 Corinthians 12:4–11.

1. What do you think each of these spiritual gifts refers to? (vv.8–10). [List gifts and explain them.] Where do these gifts come from? (v.11)

2. How do you feel about the idea of God giving us supernatural gifts?

3. Does everybody have the same gifts? (vv.4–6)
    • Different gifts, works and service, but same God

4. Why does God give spiritual gifts to people? (v.7)
    • For the common good
    • Not for our own glory

5. Mention that there will be an opportunity in the afternoon to hear more on this subject

How
can I be filled
with the
Holy Spirit

This session is followed by a time of prayer ministry in a corporate setting. Spend time praying with any guests who would like prayer to be filled with the Holy Spirit (see Training 2).

How can I make the most of the rest of my

life

Ask each member of the group, starting with the person who will be most open, to describe their experience of the weekend. This will give permission for any others who want to, to share their experiences. If appropriate you may wish to offer an opportunity for the group to pray for one another.

How can I resist

evil

Start the small group time by asking guests to share their experiences of the Alpha weekend. This gives the guests the opportunity to express what God has done in their lives. It can be a great encouragement to the group. Remember to include those who did not go on the weekend in the discussion.

QUESTIONS FOR DISCUSSION

1. Why do you think bad things happen?

2. Why do you think the world is in such a mess?

3. Before tonight, did you have a concept of the devil? Has it changed?

4. Do you believe in the supernatural/black magic/the occult?

....

....

....

....

....

....

....

....

....

....

How and why should I tell

If the dates and details of the Alpha celebration do not come up naturally in the discussion, this is a good time to mention them. Invitations can be handed out too. If possible, aim to pray together as a group at the end of this session.

QUESTIONS FOR DISCUSSION

1. Has anyone told their friends/family/colleagues at work that they are doing Alpha? What was their reaction?

2. If you did not know anything about Christianity, how would you like to be told about it?

3. What do you think/feel about the idea of telling others?

Does God heal +oday

Remind guests about the Alpha celebration. Try to work out approximately how many people will be coming, including small group members and any guests they plan to invite.

PRAYER FOR HEALING

- If words of knowledge were given at the end of the talk, ask if anyone in the group thinks that a 'word of knowledge' may have been appropriate for them

- If not, ask your guests if there is a specific problem or illness for which they would like prayer for healing. At the same time ask if anyone would like prayer for any other issue. This is a good time to clear up any general issues about healing, so allow time for the group to discuss briefly before praying together

- Pray for guests according to the prayer ministry guidelines (Training 2) in this guide. If there are lots of guests, divide into one group of men and one group of women at this stage

- Be prepared for someone who may want to give their life to Christ. Equally affirm those who do want to be prayed for and those who do not

What about the church

Remind the group about the Alpha celebration. Try to finalise numbers. Make a date for a small group reunion. This could possibly be at the host's home, ideally about two weeks before the next Alpha starts, or sooner if appropriate.

QUESTIONS FOR DISCUSSION

1. Go around the group asking each person to summarise what they have learnt and experienced over the past eleven sessions. (Try to start and finish with an enthusiastic person!)

2. Ask the group what they would like to do after Alpha. Try to encourage them to stay connected as a group

3. Ask each of them if there is anything they would like prayer for

4. Pray – it's a good idea to finish the final session with prayer

OPTIONAL QUESTIONS FOR FURTHER DISCUSSION

1. What comes to mind when you hear the words 'church' or 'Christian'?

2. Look back on the last eleven sessions. Has your view changed?

3. Looking forwards, in what way (if any) do you plan to continue what you've started on Alpha?